MW00930150

LIVING LAGOM:

A Swedish Guide to a Balanced Life

© Copyright 2018 by Maya Thoresen - All rights reserved.

The following eBook is reproduced below with the goal of providing information that is as accurate and as reliable as possible. Regardless, purchasing this eBook can be seen as consent to the fact that both the publisher and the author of this book are in no way experts on the topics discussed within, and that any recommendations or suggestions made herein are for entertainment purposes only. Professionals should be consulted as needed before undertaking any of the action endorsed herein.

This declaration is deemed fair and valid by both the American Bar Association and the Committee of Publishers Association and is legally binding throughout the United States.

Furthermore, the transmission, duplication or reproduction of any of the following work, including precise information, will be considered an illegal act, irrespective whether it is done electronically or in print. The legality extends to creating a secondary or tertiary copy of the work or a recorded copy and is only allowed with the express written consent of the Publisher. All additional rights are reserved.

The information in the following pages is broadly considered to be a truthful and accurate account of facts, and as such any inattention, use or misuse of the information in question by the reader will render any resulting actions solely under their purview. There are no scenarios in which the publisher or the original author of this work can be in any fashion deemed liable for any hardship or damages that may befall them after undertaking information described herein.

Additionally, the information found on the following pages is intended for informational purposes only and should thus be considered, universal. As befitting its nature, the information presented is without assurance regarding its continued validity or interim quality. Trademarks that are mentioned are done without written consent and can in no way be considered an endorsement from the trademark holder.

REVIEWS

Reviews and feedback help improve this book and the author. If you enjoy this book, we would greatly appreciate it if you were able to take a few moments to share your opinion and post a review on Amazon.

TABLE OF CONTENTS

CHAPTER ONE

WHAT IS LAGOM?

Lagom (pronounced [là:gɔm]) is a Swedish word used to describe the perfect state when something is neither too much, nor too little. It is just enough to make you satisfied. It can be used when talking about anything from the weather to how much milk you pour in your coffee. If the question starts with "How much?" the typical answer in Sweden is "lagom." There are a few words that can be used as synonyms for lagom; for example, enough, moderate, and balanced. Despite being perfectly good words they don't, however, correspond exactly to the true meaning of lagom as a way to express when something is just enough. Although, they might be used to create an understanding of the interpretations of lagom.

Etymologists say lagom is a composition of the two words "lag" and "om." Centuries ago, when there was a lack of food, there was only one plate containing food and had to be enough to go around the table. No one at the table could take much food. In Swedish "lag" means "team" or in this case "table" and "om" means "around." Lagom is, therefore, said to imply a meaning of *around the table.* This explanation makes sense, although, nowadays, historians and etymologists say this is a myth and perhaps have been constructed later on to explain why the Swedish used the word lagom to begin with.

Lagom is used to describe when we are satisfied, or when something is enough. We all have a different perception of when we are contempt and satisfied. The definition might be a bit difficult to define, but this is the essence of lagom. There is no general description of how much lagom is, which makes it quite a complicated word. There are as many definitions for lagom as there areSwedish. How much each one considers to be satisfying is, of course, a matter of taste, and it can be difficult even for the Swedish to understand what someone else considers to be lagom. Of course, it is a constant source of discussion amongst friends, families, and couples when one of them wants lagom and gets either too much or too little. This is due to the giver that has not bothered to ask how much the receiver consider to be lagom. It is easy to give someone else what we ourselves believe to be the right amount. Frequent misunderstandings are expected, especially in the beginning defining each other's definition and taste, according to lagom. However, the misunderstandings are neither serious nor the source of any huge conflict at all amongst the Swedish. These difficulties regarding definition are so common in Sweden that no one really thinks about it, it is a part of everyday life. And it seems that there is no real definition of the word and there lies a silent agreement the Swedish have agreed to disagree on the definition and accept that everyone thinks differently.

If there is no real definition of lagom, then why use it? Is it not confusing and weird? To non-Swedish, the definition is weird and complicated, and it can be debated whether anything is lagom. Everyone has their own definition, and it is a matter of the fact that Swedish people tend to complain more about some things, like temperature. With constant complaints about the weather being too hot or too cold, too windy or too still, too much snow or not snowy enough, it seems like there is no real use for the word lagom. At least not while talking about the Swedish topic of choice -weather.

Distinguishing lagom is like comparing food that is too hot or not hot enough; too sweet or not sweet enough; so on. Despite these constant complaints the Swedish harbor, they are quite a contempt with everything when asked seriously. Perhaps these minor complaints are a way for the Swedish people to connect to each other and start a conversation. They might be on to something. Accepting things is being lagom instead of perfect, a source of happiness some things never being quite lagom. From this aspect, it is not about a useless word, but a useful and satisfying one that makes the Swedish happy with the condition about things.

The question still remains: Why is lagom something to strive for if we are not able to agree on what lagom is?

It is complicated to see the reasons why when lagom cannot have a proper definition. But, there is one more aspect of what the point of lagom might be, we have not talked about yet. If we dropped the importance to define lagom, then the whole point is that there is *no* definition. Perhaps the whole point of lagom is to figure out what it is for you and live accordingly without being so concerned with what other people think about lagom. Let's explain this further. In Sweden, the general mentality is each to his own. In other words, don't interfere in other people's lives when they have not asked for it, like letting them express their opinions and live life on their terms. Lagom is something that needs to be figured out independently and then applied to life. There is no right or wrong definition of lagom; it is a grey middle that is defined independently and expressed differently to each person. The aspect of lagom and its definition is beautiful because it holds space for interpretation for each person.

Lagom cannot be defined as one single, universal statement,

but an independent one that each individual has to define on their own. Lagom is adaptable to life and each person and can make it entirely your own according to your beliefs without being concerned what anyone else will say. As your life and your perspective change, so can your definition of lagom. Lagom is always in tune with you.

CHAPTER TWO

LAGOM IN SWEDEN AND AROUND THE WORLD

In this second chapter, how do the Swedish people view lagom as they sometimes have a different view than the rest of the world. Since there is a difference in how the Swedish and others view lagom, let's take a closer look at these differences and the fascination of this worldwide phenomenon.

The Swedish have a somewhat complicated relationship with the word lagom and all that it stands for. The lagom lifestyle is a way of thinking and acting is deeply internalized in the Swedish way of being, and they don't tend to think about it. It is a life that goes on and on in a nice little rut of decisions, and the fact that it does makes lagom go by unnoticed, perhaps even ignored. On the contrary, other Swedish are sick and tired being labeled as lagom. They feel stuck in a rut and tend to feel ashamed being considered moderate, never too much, too loud and so on, seizing every opportunity trying to break free. It is not easy to explain why some Swedish have this feeling. Perhaps they don't want to be labeled and want to break free from the term. Others just ignore or live with the label that has been imposed on them.

Despite the anti-lagom , Swedish people, in general, are more careful to keep their lives lagom-style than living too large or putting themselves in a situation where they are noticed. The Swedish can be regarded as contempt being labeled lagom as they live their lagom lives. Perhaps some of them have become more comfortable with being lagom now when the rest of the world is picking up this trend as well. Sometimes it is easier to see the greatness once more people notice it.

The struggles with the definition mentioned in the previous chapter, the Swedish complicated relationship with this word, is a fact that many countries are becoming more and more fascinated by this phenomenon. And, it is fascinating how a rather small country like Sweden influences others to live a different kind of life in order to maintain balance. Some Swedish state that they maintain the lagom lifestyle because they find it is the easiest way to live a sustainable, healthy, happy and balanced life. Some of them consider lagom to be the perfect interstitial path in a divided world full of contradictions and non-consequent advice. Lagom allows you to enjoy all the little pleasures in life and still be healthy and satisfied.

To the rest of the world, lagom seems to be a clever way to make a difference in the world and turn certain events around in order to make things better. In a world where we face huge environmental issues and are in a constant search of ways to save the planet, lagom might, in fact, impose a more sustainable lifestyle. For example, instead of buying food that goes uneaten, buy enough to last a certain time before going grocery shopping again. This goes for clothes and everything else as well, buy what you need and what you use and leave the rest. To the rest of the world, lagom might be a way to describe that we don't want to buy more than we use and when we do buy something consider the quality over quantity aspect. This can save you time and money in the long run. This is also applicable to the work and home balance many of us struggle with. Instead of working too much and spending little time with our children, strive to do everything lagom-style to make time for both the business and pleasures in life without facing a burnout. These are some of the reasons why the world is fascinated and inspired by Sweden and lagom.

While some of the Swedish people are sick and tired of being caught in this grey scale of life where everything is lagom, in moderation and just enough to satisfy them and longing for some glamour and flair, the rest of the world are turning their eyes to Sweden as a leading example of a sustainable, healthy and happy lifestyle. So maybe the Swedish are just too self-critical and bored by the rut they are stuck in to see their own greatness and the inspiration they bring to the table and how they can actually take the lead in making things better for this planet.

CHAPTER THREE

LAGOM, HAPPINESS, AND HYGGE

We have already touched how lagom can be connected to happiness and how it can lead to a more harmonious life. In this chapter, we dig deeper in the hope of discovering more about this. In this book, when we raise the subject of lagom and its connection to happiness, keep in mind that we don't talk about happiness as this feeling in your stomach before waking up on Christmas day or hearing the footsteps outside of your door in the morning of your birthday as a child or the happiness of receiving something you have long longed for. Instead, it is a subtle and calm feeling of happiness. A happiness that does not yell at you or is overwhelming but happiness that is rising from a place of satisfaction.

Although some groups of the Swedish population are trying to break free from being labeled as lagom, Sweden has paved the way for a new way of achieving balance and also more happiness. Settling for lagom when you could be striving for more is not a bad idea. In fact, the Swedish are definitely on to something. By settling for lagom they don't take on more responsibilities than they are able to and doing so, they apply some sort of self-preservation and self-care. When settling occurs in your job and your life, there is no urgency to strive for more for yourself or for your family. Use the time to do things you enjoy that creates happiness. Working constantly is not healthy for you, your mind or your family as your energy from work has been depleted. Applying moderation in your life will create happiness and can increase the amount of happiness already present in your life.

To accomplish lagom, consider to take a look at your life and analyze what is important to you. Take a look at your habits and see how they can improve. And what better way to use some extra time than to create things that make you happy? What makes us happy is individual, but whatever you like to do, using lagom in your life will make some time for your favorite things. It is important to remember that time is not the only connection between lagom and happiness -- it is contempt. Considering things to be "just good enough" rather than striving for perfection can save plenty of irritations and help you to a stress-free life. Maybe not at first. During the first efforts of changing your way of thinking into lagom can be frustrating as things can begin to pile up and not be completed. It is like quitting smoking or caffeine. It is frustrating, and you might have abstinence from things, but after a while, happiness will come easier to you than before.

Talking about lagom and about happiness there is another phenomenon worth mentioning. In Denmark, they have a thing called hygge [pronounced hoo-ga]. Hygge can be described as a warm, cozy and comfortable atmosphere where you take your time to enjoy the good things in life with the people you love. Hygge is an activity, or a state of being, as lagom is a view on life and a way of living. However different, there is a connection to be found between hygge and lagom. They are both derived from a longing of slowing down and keeping things simple. Lagom is all about balance and moderation, and when having hygge, you are spending your time in a moderate way. It is an easy-going atmosphere where nothing is too much or too little, but just lagom. Therefore, hygge is a lagom state of being, despite the lack of connection overall. While lagom and hygge are different connections to living and feeling, they lie in cause and consequence. Applying lagom to your life to achieve balance, to find more time for the things you love to do. This extra time saved can be spent with family, friends and other loved ones, and hobbies in a cozy atmosphere called hygge. It all works out as a circle of being cozy and happy in your home as energy and money should not be wasted to enjoy the time. In other words, hygge is lagom completely.

What hygge consists of is a matter of taste. To some people it might be meeting some friends over dinner, catching up after work in a nice coffee shop or a movie night with your family. The point of hygge is to be calm and cozy, to pass the time with where you will be energized instead of burning energy constantly. Filling up your energy like this will result in a balanced, happy and content life. Furthermore, enjoying the little things in life can improve your ability to handle a mediocre job, a mean colleague at work or any other small, annoying things that occur in your everyday life.

CHAPTER FOUR

LAGOM IN PERSONAL LIFE, FAMILY, AND RELATIONSHIPS

In the first three chapters, there are many definitions of how lagom is connected to an increase in time, money and happiness in life. Discover how you can achieve these things in your life. We are going to cover the subject on how to apply lagom to your personal life, spending time with family, friends, and others, and how these actions could lead to better relationships with yourself and those around you. Plus, learn to set aside time and energy to enjoy special interests and hobbies.

Today, we are encouraged from a young age to be social; spend time with others and working well in a group is a characteristic that is encouraged and rewarded in today's society. Why this has become increasingly important is hard to find, but social skills are just as important as any other competence when looking for a job. Although, social skills and the importance of communicating well is not a new trend in itself. Guidelines for good people skills can be found in the New Testament. In Peter 4:8-9, we can find the following: "Above all, maintain constant love for one another, for love covers a multitude of sins. Be hospitable to one another without complaining". Social skills have been important for ages, but it is more important today as many people are competing for the same jobs with the same competence. With the influence of technology, online marketing and social networks online, it is even more important to stay social in order to be noticed and successful. Even during spare time, staying connected to social media isn't ideal for resting as it keeps the stress and mind alert. For some reason, being introverted and enjoying time alone and offline is almost considered a handicap, and there are even therapy and courses to teach us how to overcome this behavior and become more social. It is a challenge to stay balanced and disconnect once in a while when the world around is encouraging us to be online and connected constantly.

The Swedish, however, have a reputation of being somewhat cold and distant to strangers and to each other despite the want and need for social skills in their society. But, the Swedish are not really anti-social. Most of them are just as social as everyone else, but they inherited the mindset of leaving each to his own, combined with their lagom lifestyle, gives them an air of solitude-seeking and loneliness in their life. The Swedish behavior is actually quite healthy and something for the rest of us to adopt. In western society, we are forced to be social at work, in school and wherever we spend our time during the day. Sometimes the expectations are on high-demand for us to deliver when it comes to being social throughout the day. Spending time with family, work or study with classmates and teachers, and still expected to be cordial with our colleagues can be stressful and exhaust our energy levels. In the evening it is still expected from others and society to be social on days off when all our bodies need is sleep and rest. Filling up days things to do within the week leads to exhaustion and lost interests and passions in life. When transitioning to the lagom lifestyle, you might get frustrated and even hate doing things you usually enjoy with others just because you have been forced into everything and forced away from yourself.

Therefore, it is important to keep in touch with yourself and your own interests in order to enjoy all of these social events that are quite nice when you find the balance.

In Sweden, when people sit alone on the bus or avoid talking to each other while waiting in line at the supermarket, they are creating a balance between social commitments recovery time. It is true that the Swedish are keener on minding their own business than many others and contributes to their lagom lifestyle. They can chat with the person next to them, but they don't because of value space and privacy. In these situations, lagom does not mean staying at the house, locking yourself inside and have scheduled time alone because that does not work. Instead, lagom is about being quiet while riding the bus or standing in line. It is not the perfect scheduled downtime alone but rather a good compromise to recharge and have more energy once you get home to your family. By applying lagom this way, the Swedish have cracked the code of balance between being social and being alone. Instead of bending over backward trying to keep up with all the social events and commitments, the Swedish people take care of their alone time. They spend time alone by themselves or with their family allowing the time to recover and recharge. Because being social can lead to frustration and exhaustion.

Once you take the time to rearrange your busy schedule and recharge properly, it is possible that you will want to take up a hobby. Hobbies are often the first to get crossed of the lists as we become busy with work and family. Although, hobbies are good for the well-being and having a thing you love is relaxing and recharging in itself. As discussed earlier, applying lagom leads to an increased amount of free time that you can use to recharge. Recharging energy levels can bring love and joy to the hobbies once loved. The love and joy you find in a hobby also generate new energy that you need for work and family. Of course, a hobby can be social, but by being alone, you can do only what you feel like. Your mind can rest for a moment, and you can go deep within and follow your voice. Lagom is about balance, and if you are usually very social, this is a way to find balance.

On the other hand, if you are anti-social and prefer spending time alone, lagom might mean that you should put yourself out there more. Maybe create time to spend with friends, family, and others. If you are generally anti-social at work, try talking to your colleagues and ask them questions to spark conversation. Meeting new people outside of work like joining a group or join an association to share like-minded interests. Meeting new people can bring fulfillment in life and enjoy life experiences.

Finding a balance between work and home life can be hard to accomplish but is completely possible. If you find yourself working yourself hard with no time left for pleasure or find yourself complaining about the workload, then you might want to take a look at the solution you are able to control. The solution may not always be there, but by thinking about your options and asking friends, family or co-workers for help, a solution will arise. If you can, maybe talk to your boss about having too much on your hands, say no to colleagues who want help when you are too busy for your own work. Or, help each other out to succeed at the same goal. If you find that you are working at a dead-end, try to find a new job or a new career. Everything is possible to achieve balance in your life.

Sorting out your priorities can be hard. To find the lagom balance, write a list of things you feel like you have to do and write a list of things you want to enjoy doing. Then, prioritize the list of things you have to do and would like to do, putting them in order starting with the most important. Throughout the day, cross them off as you go. The key here is doing a little of what has to be done and would like to enjoy doing. At the end of the day, both lists will have things crossed off to see what was accomplished. This will leave you feeling satisfied and contempt how the day was spent. In other words, doing more with the time you have to enjoy a moment of hygge with family and friends.

The Swedish are not better than anyone else at saying no, prioritizing and enjoying relationships and hobbies. Although they do have the concept of lagom, they don't think about what they can do on their days off to spend time with their families and friends. Perhaps the Swedish have a more natural longing for solitude than others, helping them to stay balanced in their social engagements.

Lagom is a lifestyle to achieve balance within yourself and in your life. Spending time with family and friends and enjoying hobbies and interests alone is important to your health and mind. Do everything well enough instead of striving for perfection; no one will thank you for working yourself hard than settling for a little less. Do not feel guilty for not giving your all and most important think of lagom in the sense of doing everything in moderation and for balance. If you have worked too much, then make sure to spend some time at home, if you have been social a lot then try to have some alone time. And so on.

How much should you have of everything in order to have balance? Depends how much you should work, be alone, socialize, etc. is up to you to decide. If you love your job and don't have anyone waiting at home, then spend more time at work. If you recharge by being surrounded by people, then spend more time with others while an introvert may need more time alone to feel balanced. Think about your wants, needs and what you have to do and see what can be rearranged to achieve that balance in life the lagom way. Everything in moderation and remember that a little of everything is better than nothing of some and too much of others.

CHAPTER FIVE

LAGOM AT HOME

Lagom is not only useful for creating harmony and balance between work and life or between socializing and time alone; it is a useful tool to make your home a peaceful, relaxing and comfortable space to dwell in. In this chapter, focus on creating the most peaceful home you have ever had the lagom way.

Starting with the home itself and its decorations, there are a plethora of things to make it a cozy and comfortable place to be. Do you have any furniture not being used by you, your family, or guests? Start with that. Filter out the furniture that is never used to eliminate the clutter and fill your home with decorations you love, and that brings you joy and happiness. Then continue on, eliminating decorations, cushions, and curtains you don't like, use or fit in your home.

Home is a place to relax, spend time with your family and escape from all your social engagements, work, and demands from people outside. Having a home that has things you love it can bring joy, confidence, and happiness to you and others around you. Having a cluttered home can be overwhelming, which can bring stress to your life instead of relaxation. Remember that you owe your things, not the other way around.

The moment your things become cluttered, and they serve no

use to you or the house's function, it is time to start decluttering and achieve Zen. Zen is an eastern philosophy that originated in Buddhism. In our western culture, it has come to reflect a calm and meditative state of being. There is no obvious connection between lagom and Zen, but when applying lagom and decluttering your home, you can reach a calm and satisfying state where you owe your things without being overwhelmed. When reaching Zen by living lagom, you will also feel more energized and less stressed. Despite the lack of connection between this two phenomenon and philosophies, lagom is a useful technique if you want to achieve zen. In search of a peaceful, happy and rich life, lagom, as well as zen, are powerful tools to use. Furthermore, Zen is a well-known and popular philosophy, and by connecting lagom to Zen and letting them work together, may give a wider perspective in the world.

When it comes to things, it is not better to have more. In fact, many things only give you more to clean, more to replace when broken or worn out and you will probably spend more time searching for things you have replaced and cannot find anymore. You should absolutely have what you need, but don't fill your home with nice things only to have them full or to show off to occasional visitors. Instead, try to adopt a less is more approach to your home. How much things your home should contain is up to you as it is a matter of need and taste. Feel free to have curtains, cushions, a wine glass collection and those nice and expensive dinner plates you only use for Christmas, but take a look at your life and what you really need, what you think you need, and how much of everything you need. Don't forget to only keep and buy things you truly love and care for. Even if you need an item, don't keep it if it does not make you smile. Sell the old one, or give it away and invest in a piece that makes you smile instead. Remember, the definition of lagom is up to you and differ from person to person.

Many people say they need more storage space or smart solutions to store things in the already existing storage areas of their homes, but what most people actually need is to clean out their spaces and sort out what to keep and what to get rid of. A home that is cluttered-free is more harmonious, and you can come home from work feeling relaxed and comfortable instead of your home flooded with things you need to organize and clean. Of course, decluttering your home takes work, and it can take a long time before you are completely done, but once your home is properly organized and neat, you will find yourself at peace. There is always something to declutter like that junk draw in the kitchen or bedroom, or underneath the sinks are perfect places to clean out and organize. Who knows, the process could become a hobby you enjoy to do.

Another cluttered mess that can impact the home environment and your life is your wardrobe. Getting dressed in the morning can be both pleasure and torture. Many of us are sick and tired of looking at our clothes and thinking that we have nothing to wear. Decluttering your wardrobe the lagom way can get rid of this anxiety-driven nightmare.

Begin by emptying your closet. This is not something you have to do; it is recommended to see the clothes you have and get a good picture of the state your current wardrobe is in. Then, pick up one item at the time and consider how much you like this item, how much you can identify with it and how useful it is in your everyday life. Only keep the things you use, love and feel are right for you. It is not necessary to make it into a complete capsule wardrobe with a limited amount of pieces. The point is to keep it organized and simple so that you have a wardrobe that expresses your personality and where you can easily find the perfect combination for each occasion, where the clothes fit together nicely and are made in materials of good quality.

After you have organized your current wardrobe and gotten rid of things you don't want, write a list of things you need to complement the rest of your wardrobe. Another great tip regarding clothes and is easy, plan out your outfits for the week ahead saving you time and agony in the morning. The Swedish uses lagom to simplify their wardrobe and their lives as they have more time making and eating a nice breakfast instead.

We have talked about our homes and wardrobes, but how can you shop the lagom way? The Swedish love to shop, but they are conscious buyers. Being a conscious buyer is to buy only what you need, considering quality over quantity and always follow your taste. The perfect way to buy what you only need is making a list. It does not matter if you are buying decorations for your home, clothes or food --think about what you need and write a list (the Swedish love lists). Also, avoid impulse buying. If faced with a situation where you are standing in a store wanting to buy something, consider its use in your life. If you cannot come up with one, walk away. Also, think about quality over quantity so items can last longer when it comes to clothes, furniture, and decorations. This way you buy fewer things you will enjoy for a longer time.

When shopping with moderation, think twice before buying anything. It may seem dull to shop the lagom way, but it can be delightful spending time looking for one perfect, thoughtful item then multiple not-so-good items. This will save you time and money, and become happier with each buy than before. Before shopping, consider the following questions:

- Do I need this item?
- When will I use it? Think of at least one specific moment in the near-future when you will wear or use this item.

- Can I afford this? Don't consider the price tag; consider how many times you can wear or use this piece. An expensive thing can cost less than a budget alternative if used more frequently than the cheaper option.
- Do I want this for myself or is it something I want because everyone else has it? Only buy things you want; don't buy anything because someone else says so.
- Do I already have this or something similar at home to use instead?
- Will I be able to sell this when I no longer find it useful? Even if you are uncertain about a buy, determine if it can be resold later on. By selling things for someone else to use saves money and incorporates sustainable living habits.

Sometimes an impulse can meet the criteria's of a good bargain. If faced with an impulse buy, after using the questions above, use this trick: Take a picture of it. Go home and sleep on it. If you are still thinking about the item can envision its functionality in your home or life, then can buy it. Most of the time we don't crave these impulses the next day, but if we do, it may be a good item to buy.

Buying the lagom way can bring happiness, joy, and comfort to you and others around you. Less things mean more space and time. More space means that your home will be easier to clean and to keep things tidy on a daily basis. Now, you will have more time for other hobbies or interests because you're not spending time cleaning. A wardrobe that is simple and easier to choose from will leave more time and energy for the day. Less things mean more money. Selling the things you don't want to keep and earn extra money is sustainable. Decluttering your home will make it appear open, neat, and clean for guests and yourself.

All of these things save you energy and time doing things you love with the people you love. Declutter, stay organized and find suitable solutions to keep your habitat tidy to turn your home into a relaxing and calm place where you find peace and recharge.

CHAPTER SIX

LAGOM HEALTH
AND WELL BEING

Discussing the impact of lagom when applying it to relationships, life, and home can help decrease stress and increase time, money and energy for things you want to enjoy. Lagom is not always about the materialistic relics in your home or how you feel in social outings; it can affect how you feel within yourself: your well-being.

In Sweden, people like to move their bodies not because they need to achieve anything but because of how it makes them feel both in their mind and in their bodies. They love the feeling of movement in their bodies, which is one more reason for them to exercise. Swedish people might not be known for being the most competitive people when it comes to sports, but they do move frequently. They exercise everyday like taking walks and riding bikes instead of driving. They take the stairs instead of the elevator, and so on. The Swedish like to keep their bodies healthy. Marathon training, Viking races, and iron man races have become a trend lately for even the average Swede. Although these races are rather extreme, they have become increasingly popular, and it is a sign of the current trends. Despite the Swedish fascination for exercise and the impact it has on the body and mind, they are cautious not to overdo anything. Instead of exercising way too much for the perfect body, they work out in order to achieve the accomplishment itself and for the feel of it.

But not all Swedish are interested in these extreme workouts, and even those who are dedicated to them are careful not to stretch their bodies too much. They are careful to have lagom and balance between working out their bodies, their minds and relaxing all together. Exercising is something that needs fit into the work and life balance, and this can be challenging. To maintain a balance between activity and rest as well as between work and life and instead of having only the toughest workouts, they go for a hike in the forest for a day or do something else that balances exercise with family life while still bringing tranquility. You can definitely have a balance and still keep up with an exercise routine.

Hiking and doing things with your family can be considered relaxing while still being physical activity. It is relaxing because you don't just work your body, your brain gets a mental rest while enjoying a hygge moment with family in the forest or by the sea. This can also aid in recovery and boost energy levels.

In general, the Swedish love spending time in nature. It does not matter if they are going for a run, spending the day with their kids in the park or spending sunny summer days by the sea swimming and tanning. Spending time outside can boost your body in more than one way with staying active and delivering much-needed vitamins to the skin. Most of the time we are indoors working, studying, or spending time alone or with others, we forget how much our bodies need to stay active.

Health and well-being are not all about physical exercise. It is relaxing and exercises the mind. We spend our days with a lot of impressions, and it is hard sometimes to tune out and let the mind rest for a moment. In Sweden, meditation, mindfulness, and yoga have become increasingly popular in order to balance the hectic life. Not everyone loves meditation, and all people certainly don't love yoga, but the fine thing is that doing what the Swedish do when being in nature, saying no to certain events to be with family and recover is to be considered mindfulness and gives life a nice touch of lagom.

Another movement in Sweden where more and more people are moving to the countryside, buying a cabin outside of town and gardening has kicked up popularity and can be relaxing and satisfying for the mind. This can be considered a reaction to make the hectic life more lagom. There are several ways to create balance and find some peace of mind in our daily lives. Remember, lagom everything.

Closely related to the subject of health and exercise is what you eat. As far as food is considered, the Swedish try to prioritize eating solid home-cooked meals made with clean and healthy ingredients as possible. They prefer to eat with their families, and to most people in Sweden, good food is important to the overall well-being. They do eat junk food moderately but shy away from microwaveable dinners or anything containing chemicals. They use real butter despite the calories than eating light products that contain additives that are generally not good for your health. It is easy to find and buy organic food, and they are dedicated to buying locally produced food to support small businesses and avoid the long transportations of food. Food transportations take time so that the food is not fresh once it reaches the store. The transportations contribute to pollution, and the Swedish prefer to buy local. Locally produced food is like a quality stamp that guarantees the food is of good quality, costing more than average, the Swedish like to support their local farmers. They love to eat good food, but in the true sense of lagom they do not only want it to taste good, but they also want it to be healthy.

In Sweden, the National Food Agency (NFA), provides guidelines on how to eat to get all of the important nutrients the body needs. It is a discussion amongst the Swedish if they should be trusted or not since some of their advice is contradictory to certain peoples believes regarding what is to be considered healthy food. This is not a proven fact, but in Sweden, people following specific diets, for example, Paleo and LCHF dislike that the NFA recommends the Swedish to eat plenty of pasta, bread, and other carbs. Some trust them, and some don't, but whether you trust these guidelines or not, they are created to help people live healthy lives, by recommending a diet containing both vegetables, fruits, carbs, fats, and proteins. The NFA guidelines state to fill at least a third of your plate (preferably half of it) with vegetables and/or fruits. But, the Swedish love their traditional dishes. They are also curious about trying new things and are not afraid to mix things up with influences from different corners of the world.

Finding healthy food that is not chemically treated, organic and locally produced is easy in Sweden. You can find these foods both in the local supermarkets and in local farmers markets. If you are insecure or don't have time to grocery shop, they have different websites like Blue Apron and Hello Fresh, where you can order your groceries online to be delivered straight home along with healthy recipes. There is something to fit every food choices in your life: vegan food, vegetarian, easy to cook food, and grocery bags with organic food if you would prefer that. The Swedish people strive to live the lagom way regarding their health. And if you might find these concepts new and time-consuming, the Swedish people do it quite effortlessly since they incorporate several of these things together. For example, they relax from work by spending time outside with their families, and while doing this, they get exercise, relaxation and family time all wrapped up in one. They cook a delicious and healthy meal and eat with their family. As a bonus, to make it easier for you to start living the lagom way, there recipes in the next chapter.

CHAPTER SEVEN

LAGOM IN THE KITCHEN

To continue the health and lifestyle the lagom way, here are some classical Swedish recipes to try at home. As an added bonus, we included some non-Swedish recipes that they love and fit their lagom lifestyle. There will be tips on how to make your own junk food, since making things yourselves will make it healthier, and you can add healthy choices to otherwise unhealthy meals. This way you will get a nice overall view of how lagom can be applied practically to all aspects of life.

Before we get started, it is necessary to point out these recipes have been slightly altered. We had added some veggies to classical recipes because when these dishes became popular, the Swedish did not have access to many vegetables due to the cold and difficult climate. Today, fruits and vegetables are imported, and the use of greenhouses have become popular that access to these ingredients is easier to obtain than ever before. The Swedish now eat more veggies, salads, and fruits along with their meats and starches. With that said, the traditional recipes are not really healthy and have been adapted as access to vegetables and other ingredients have become easier to obtain.

There are a few recipes for breakfast, lunch, and dinner that the Swedish love to eat. As a bonus, we will share tips for healthier desserts and snacks the Swedish people love.

BREAKFAST

Breakfast is considered the most important meal, especially in Sweden. It is common to eat cereals or granola with milk or yogurt, sandwiches, and porridge. Although there has been an increasing trend in eating overnight oats or drinking a smoothie, the traditional breakfast dishes are still the most popular ones. Here we share a recipe for simple granola that you can add your favorite flavors too and modify to your taste. You also get easy to make oatmeal porridge that will give you enough energy to last all the way to lunch without having your blood sugar levels sinking too low.

Homemade granola with yogurt

Ingredients

Mixed nuts (neutral, not roasted or salted)
Oatmeal
Coconut flakes
Flaxseed

Sunflower seed
Honey or maple syrup
Olive oil
Cinnamon
Cardamom

Directions

1. Mix all the dry ingredients together on an ovenproof dish.
2. Mix in some olive oil and honey or maple syrup.
3. Season it and let it dry in the oven at a low temperature during 30-45 minutes, don't forget to open the oven and mix the granola a couple of times while it is drying. Otherwise, it might burn on top and still be moist in the bottom.

If you are allergic to nuts, you can add some other grains and seeds. If you don't like cinnamon or cardamom, you can use other spices of your choice. Leave to cool down before putting it in a jar. Add dried fruits such as raisins, apricots or cranberries once the granola is dried and cold for a fruity flavor and added benefits.

Oatmeal porridge

Ingredients

 1 part oatmeal
 2 parts water
 A pinch of salt

Directions

This one is so easy it is fail-proof, and anyone can do it.

1. Take one part oatmeal and two parts water, add a pinch of salt and cook until the porridge is firm but not glue-like. If it is too lose then cook it some more; if it is too hard or has the same texture as glue, add more water and stir.
2. Serve the porridge with fresh fruits and berries and milk, if you like. Use almond milk, coconut milk, or lactose-free milk for a dairy-free alternative.

SANDWICHES

If you-you'd a sandwich eater for breakfast, here are some healthier lagom alternatives. In fact, the sandwich is not a bad option since it is versatile and you can make anything with a sandwich. Use sourdough bread and fill it with a wide range of healthier options like hummus or cream cheese instead of butter topped with your favorite vegetables. Or, use a cream cheese spread and add cold chicken, some green leafs such as spinach leaves or arugula leaves, tomato with a yogurt dressing to make it moist. The options are endless.

If you prefer having eggs in the morning eat up. Eggs are an excellent source of protein and good fats. Plus, the Swedish eat a ton of eggs, boiled or fried, or poached to put on a sandwich. They also eat scrambled eggs and bacon for breakfast at times. Keep lagom in mind and eat everything in moderations; there really are no other rules here.

LUNCH AND DINNER

For lunch, the Swedish usually have leftovers from dinner the night before as they cook huge meals during the weekends and store the leftovers in the freezer or fridge to eliminate cooking lunch during the weekdays. Of course, some eat lunch out, but the average Swedish person brings leftovers to work. The Swedish children are served lunch in school, so they don't have to bring their own, but during weekends and holidays, the families usually eat a cooked meal at home. The lunch and dinner dishes are similar to all of these recipes can be served as either lunch or dinner. Of course, the Swedish do eat out, but not on a regular basis. In Sweden, eating out is to celebrate and indulge themselves than that is part of everyday life.

Classic Swedish Meatballs

This has to be the most famous and popular dish amongst Swedish recipes, and we could not leave this one out. It is a classic favorite dish in Sweden for a reason. Try it, and you will understand why. It is easy to make, tasty, and kids will love. Add vegetables for added health benefits.

Ingredients

The minced meat of your choice (beef, pork, or lamb)	Breadcrumbs
	Milk
	Butter or olive oil
Onion	Salt
Egg	Pepper

Directions

1. Mix the breadcrumbs with the milk and leave it to settle.
2. Chop or grate the onion into fine pieces.
3. Mix minced meat with the onion, egg, salt, and pepper. Mix it all together with a spoon or your hands.
4. Pour in some of the milk and breadcrumbs mixes and mix it in the meat. Keep adding milk and breadcrumbs until the blend has a nice texture. It should be soft to roll and the meatballs firm. Try to frying a meatball to see how it cooks. If it is too dry, it will crumble. Add more milk and breadcrumbs to the mixture.
5. Fry the meatballs in butter.

Serve the meatballs with boiled or mashed potatoes and brown sauce. Traditional meatballs are served with pickled cucumbers and lingonberry jam with grilled tomato, a mixed salad on the side, green beans, peas or broccoli.

Steak with oven roasted potatoes and béarnaise sauce

Another classic dish in Sweden that is popular in the summertime when you can have a barbecue, but it is also possible to make it inside the stow. This one is also easy to make.

Ingredients

A steak of your choice	Potatoes
Béarnaise (Homemade is	Olive oil
preferred but bought one	Salt
is nice also)	Pepper

Directions

1. Cut the potatoes in two or four, and season with olive oil, salt, pepper, and French herbs. Roast in the oven, 225 °C for about 30 minutes.

2. Season the steak with salt and pepper. Grill or fry steak.

Serve the steak with the béarnaise sauce and roasted potatoes. Serve with in-season vegetables along with grilled (or fried) tomatoes, asparagus or green beans. Add a mixed salad on the side, grilled (or fried) corn-cob or anything else you and your family like.

Homemade Béarnaise Sauce

Ingredients

2 Egg yolks	Pepper
Red wine vinegar	Estragon
100-gram butter	Parsley
Salt	

Directions

1. Mix egg yolks with some red wine vinegar.
2. Melt the butter and leave to rest.
3. Heat the eggs in a bowl above boiling water. Whisk it constantly.

When the eggs start to thicken, remove it from the heat and start adding the butter a little at the time while whisking constantly. When the sauce is nice and thick (you might not need all the butter) you add salt, pepper, and the herbs according to your taste.

Pasta carbonara

While pasta dishes are primarily Italian, but Swedish recipes have adopted them into their meals. A dish is pasta carbonara. This is not the actual original Italian recipe but is used in Sweden and can be altered to your tastes. Feel free to add more garlic, remove the parsley, use the entire egg instead of just the yolk and so on. Nothing can wrong in this recipe.

Ingredients

Spaghetti noodles
Bacon
Cream (start with 1
deciliter and add more if
you want more sauce)
Onion

Garlic
Salt
Pepper
Parsley
Egg yolk

Directions

1. Boil the spaghetti.
2. Chop the onion, garlic, and bacon and fry together.
3. Add cream and seasonings.
4. Mix the spaghetti and egg yolk together with the bacon and cream mixture. Let it simmer. If you want more sauce, just add more cream.

Serve pasta on top of spinach leaves and add a side dish of chopped tomatoes with olive oil and salt.

Paned plaice file with mashed potatoes

Of course, we cannot exclude fish from the menu since Swedish people eat plenty of seafood. The key to all fish is to keep it simple. Like this plaice file. It is easy and tasty and most certainly a fail-proof dish to serve. If you can, try to get some fresh fish instead of frozen as it changes the taste entirely.

Ingredients

Plaice file (fresh or
frozen)
Breadcrumbs
Egg

Potatoes
Milk
Butter

Directions

1. Beat the eggs in a bowl until blended together. Set aside.
2. Coat the plaice files in the egg mixture and bread it in the breadcrumbs; cover completely.
3. Fry the files in butter , about 3-5 minutes on each side.
4. Boil the potatoes and mash them with milk and butter to taste.

Serve the fish and mash potatoes with a slice of lemon and a mixed salad of your choice. We recommend green peas, Brussels sprouts, broccoli or if you have it at home you can serve it with ratatouille.

Toast Skagen

This toast is more of an entree dish, and it is so delicious we could not possibly leave it out. Skagen is a place located on the Swedish west coast, but it is unclear why this particular dish was named after it, perhaps it has something to do with the west coast in Sweden is most famous for its seafood. However, this toast is a delicacy served not only in the west coast but in restaurants all over Sweden.

Ingredients

Fresh shrimps, peeled	Crème Fraîche
Dill	Bread (preferably
Lemon	sourdough, but any kind
Horseradish	that you can fry will do)
Mayonnaise	A slice of butter

Directions

1. Mix the shrimps with dill, grated horseradish, mayonnaise and crème fraîche, all according to your liking.
2. Season with salt, pepper, and lemon to taste. Add more

seasoning if needed.

3. Fry the bread in the butter until it is golden brown. If the bread is soaking up the butter, add more. The pan is not supposed to run dry; this will burn the bread instead.

4. Put the mixture shrimps on the bread. Decorate the toast with a dill twig and a slice of lemon.

A few classical Swedish dishes that will make you satisfied without being too much. They are delicious and easy to make with the capability to add more vegetables for added health benefits. By trying out these recipes, it is easy to understand why the Swedish have extra time to do all the things they want and need to do to achieve lagom in their lives. These recipes are simple to prepare and cook, leaving more time for family than in the kitchen.

JUNK FOOD

The fact is that junk food cannot be completely erased out of our diets, even the Swedish. And we cannot write about lagom and food without mentioning junk food. How can enjoy junk food in a lagom way while still maintaining a healthy diet and lifestyle. Here are some tips that the Swedish use.

First and foremost try to keep the balance. If you eat healthy and well balanced most of the time, there is no reason why you should not enjoy junk food every once in a while. By all means, indulge yourself in a burger, fries and a milkshake moderately. Use the Swedish model of dining out and do it to spoil yourself instead of using fast food as a go to, everyday solution than cooking at home. We know that many junk food restaurants have begun serving healthier options, like carrot sticks instead of fries. But even in Sweden, the fries with the burger is a love relationship that can't be separated. The healthy and conscious

Swedish have figured out that if they eat healthy all the other days, they can enjoy junk food. Just don't let it happen on a daily basis.

Furthermore, burgers and pizza can be made at home and are easy to prepare. Even French fries can be healthy if made at home as the salt is controlled than at a fast-food place. Make sure to use clean ingredients without bad supplements or chemicals, and try to make the majority of the sauces and dough (for pizza) yourself. A homemade burger with pineapple, pickled onions, salad, and tomato, is not so bad. Besides, making them yourself will make you feel fuller faster and control how much you intake. Making your own fries by cutting potatoes and baking them with olive oil and salt in the oven instead of buying fries is a better and healthier alternative.

Making your own pizza is a healthier option, choosing fresh ingredients and control what goes in and on your pizza. Plus, it is a fun activity for the whole family to enjoy together.

It can be overwhelming cooking at home on most nights, but it is well worth the effort. In Sweden, gathering a few friends or family and cooking together is a great way to socialize.

SNACKS

In Sweden, it is recommended to eat three larger meals and two snacks each day. Eating breakfast, lunch, and dinner, plus two snacks between lunch and dinner. This helps regulate blood sugar levels to help maintain energy all day, eliminating the two o'clock crash and cravings. So, what is the Swedish snack of choice? It depends who you are asking and how old they are.

The younger children have something called a "fruit break" at school in the morning. Each child will have brought the fruit of choice in their school bag and eat their fruit as a class. Even at home, most children are served a fruit when they crave a little something between meals. Sometimes the children are served plain yogurt along with the fruit to keep the hunger at bay a while longer if needed.

For adults, two snacks are not necessary, and most will not eat that much. The adults who do eat two snacks in-between meals will eat a fruit or plain yogurt with fruit like the children. Other common snacks are a boiled egg, served with ham or another source of protein and/or a healthy sandwich. A smaller portion of the breakfast eaten as a snack or maybe a smoothie instead are popular options for a snack. The best of all is that these are all healthy and good options instead of consuming chocolate, a cookie or other sugary options. Of course, if you really crave a piece of chocolate, you can totally have a bite of that too. Just do it like the Swedish and choose at least 70% dark chocolate every so often; not every day.

It is about the balance when eating or adopting a lagom lifestyle. These changes will help you make better choices in more than one way. Snacking should be easy and easy to carry around with you, access it, and eat wherever.

The Swedish also enjoy coffee, in a lagom way. Drinking too much coffee is not good, but in Sweden, it is the obvious drink of choice even during snack time. So if you want to try snacking the Swedish style, combine healthy options with coffee, and you are on your way to eating the lagom way.

CHAPTER EIGHT

LAGOM AS A WAY OF SAVING THE PLANET

We have covered how lagom is applied in most Swedish homes and how you can use it to change your life. The question lies: How does the lagom lifestyle impacts on a global level? The lagom way might help save our planet by living more modest lives and, therefore, respecting our nature and switching to a more ecological life. The lagom lifestyle suggests you are conscious of your environment and the impact your habits have on it. Just as you strive for doing everything in moderation, take into account how it can moderate impact on the planet and its environment like increasing pollution, damaging ecosystems with littering, or anything else that can harm the planet. In this chapter, we will discover what you can do to lead a better, environmental-friendly life.

The lagom lifestyle is closely connected to conscious habits and buying the things needed and used for functionality instead of impulse buying on a want basis. When we spend our money on things we were taught to believe we should want. We are told by various ads in papers, magazines and on billboards, and TV commercials to want all sorts of different things for ourselves, our homes and our children. But, that can be further from the truth.

Most often, we don't consider the materials or sustainability that are used on the things we buy. This includes items we buy just to sit in the closet or in a drawer that will eventually be thrown out adding to the landfills and trash in the oceans than recycling them. By applying the lagom way in your lives and focusing on building a sustainable life than consumption will bring awareness how money is being spent and why. The Swedish are actually one of the most environmental-friendly countries to live in, and there is much the rest of us can learn from that.

When buying something, anything at all, to consider not only the quality of the things but what materials are used and how it's produced. Pick a material that will last a lifetime and produced in a conscious way. Look for different labels such as eco, cruelty-free or fair trade. There are several different labels like this, and they could vary depending on what country you live in. Read different certificates in your country or state, and what they mean and try to buy things that are produced that way. This will make an impact on the environment, as well as for the people producing them. For example, buying eco coffee means that the people working in the fields work environments are healthier, pay is within the state or country regulations, and so on. Stay conscious of what you buy and how it affects other people. We are all not perfect, including the Swedish, but practice the lagom way often and question why you are buying things, what materials are used, and is it sustainable for long-term usage. For example, watch out for materials in clothes that contain micro-plastics that wash out into the ocean during washing, or switch your ordinary coffee to an ecological brand instead. The taste will be better, that is a promise.

Before buying anything new, determine if you could find the same item at a thrift store or estate sale. Vintage has always been a thing in Sweden and particularly now it is a trend on the rising, where young people buy clothes and furniture from shops, spending time altering the clothes or items to personalize it.

If you do buy new clothes, try to buy brands of good quality that will last throughout time. This is particularly useful for the basics in your wardrobe, like the items used on a daily basis such as shirts, pants, jeans and so on. The Swedish prioritize a classical wardrobe so they can invest in high-quality items than buying multiple cheap items that will have to be replaced each season when they become out of date.

In Sweden, many are moving to the countryside away from the hustle and bustle of the city. Although there are many new homes being built, many choose to buy older homes outside the cities and villages. Many spend their time and money restoring the homes instead of building new homes in these areas, being environmentally-conscious to how new homes can affect the planet. Restoring homes can lead a satisfying effect on your body and mind, and rejuvenate new life into older homes that would have eventually been torn down.

Being environmentally-friendly and conscious, many Swedish have been growing their own plants, vegetables, and fruits in their backyards or balconies. Growing your own food is a huge trend that can save you money. Another added benefit is getting your hands dirty with Mother Nature, which is good for the mind and soul, and provide quality time with yourself and your family. Remember to be lagom and incorporate low maintenance plants like tomatoes, berry bushes, or flowers that require little attention and time. Growing your garden can help improve the quality of air around you, outside and inside your home. There are many benefits incorporating nature in your home and surroundings. While other people are stressed in the cities, making changes in your life can help the planet while finding peace at the same time.

There are, however, many things you can do to live the lagom way and saving the planet that doesn't involve moving or changing your shopping habits. In Sweden, things like plastic reduction, recycling, and zero waste efforts are popular in the lagom lifestyle to living a moderate life, which might include reducing the impact we make on the environment. As a way to minimize this, bring reusable bags to the supermarket, buy sustainable, quality clothes, and minimize your waste. Also, the Swedish people love to recycle almost everything such as plastic, paper, glass bottles, and tin cans and so on, as another way to do what is best for the planet.

CHAPTER NINE

21-DAY LAGOM CHALLENGE

We will wrap this book up with twenty-one different challenges to give the Swedish lifestyle a chance and find out if it is a fit for you. Challenge yourself to adopt the lagom lifestyle and have an open mind. Be sure to track your progress in a journal during 21-days to see your progress and what works for you and your family. Some of the challenges will see huge and need more time than just a day to adjust, but choose a small area of your life or home to change and narrow it down little by little. Once you feel confident with a change, continue on with another change until the lagom lifestyle is achieved.

Here's a list to help aid you on your way to achieving the lagom way:

1.Hygge

Instead of attending or hosting a party, meet up with your closest friends and have some hygge time. This might include something simple as a good cup of coffee at a local coffee shop or having a simple dinner at home. The possibilities are endless.

2. Self-care

Schedule some alone time today and do something that recharges your batteries. It could be a walk in the forest or a trail, a bubble bath or staying in bed reading a book for a while in the morning or in the evening. The key is to find tranquility with yourself.

3. Spend time in nature

Get outside and enjoy what's around you. Take a walk, ride your bike or do anything to get you moving. Spending time close to nature is good for your body and soul.

4. Try something new

Why not try a new hobby today. Do something you don't think you'll enjoy doing. You might be surprised. Or, do something that you are afraid of doing skydiving or going to a new town to explore. J If you feel uncomfortable doing it yourself, bring a friend.

5. Take up an old hobby

Rekindle those old hobbies you use to enjoy. Sometimes we quit doing things without even knowing why or when life gets too busy. This will help find peace and tranquility with yourself and your life.

6. Say no

Today's challenge is to say no to something. The Swedish are people pleasers, but they are will say no to things they don't have the time for or feel like doing. Say no to something today, and you'll be surprised at how calm you may feel afterward. Remember, you can't do everything every time for everyone.

7. Settle for good enough

If you are a perfectionist, this will be hard. Sometime today, when you are performing a task, challenge yourself to leave your task once it is done. If you have done it properly, consider it done if it is good enough even if you don't find it perfect. Try it and see what happens. If you don't feel comfortable doing this at work, try at home. When cleaning, settle when it is clean even if there still might be some little thing left to clean. Don't overexert yourself to get things accomplish perfectly each time. No one will probably notice the small imperfection anyway.

8. Declutter your home

Choose a room or small space to start the decluttering process. Do not take on your whole home as it will become overwhelming and discouraging. Tackle a drawer, a cupboard, or closet first, even your desk, to declutter and open up space. Ask yourself questions to assess in the decluttering process:

- Do I use this item on a regular basis?
- Do I need this item (if yes, make sure you know what you need it for)?
- Do I love this item (does it spark joy)?
- Do I need more of this? (Ask this question if you already have multiple similar items).

Only keep the things you use and need. Not all items are useful, some are only decorations and can stay as long as you like the item and as long as it has a given place.

Once you are done, organize what is left and get rid of the clutter through donation or reselling.

9. Declutter and organize your wardrobe

Go through your closet and get rid of the things you no longer use or like. Instead of throwing them out, donate them or sell online. After you have decided what will stay, go ahead and organize your wardrobe, so it is easy to find everything. If this challenge seems too hard becomes overwhelming, narrow it down. Choose one area to begin with like cleaning out your underwear drawer and organize it properly. Then continue on with the rest another day.

10. Choose outfits for a week ahead

Organizing your clothes is one step. Today, plan out your outfits for the week ahead and stick to them. If this seems overwhelming, plan a few days ahead until it becomes a habit you enjoy doing. Planning outfits in advance can save time in the morning and energy. Your clothes are put together already making getting dressed easy and efficient in the morning.

11. Go vintage shopping

Go vintage shopping. Shopping at thrift stores and online helps recycle older clothes and adds personality to your wardrobe and home with unique and one-of-a-kind items. If you don't find the perfect thing, use your imagination and see if you can find something that is easy to alter and incorporate it in your home or wardrobe.

12. Exercise outside

Leave the gym and take your exercise outside. Take in the fresh air and all the benefits of being outdoors. You don't need much equipment or special workout clothes. Lace up your running shoes, comfortable clothes, and go for a brisk walk or run. Feel the need for some strength training? Stop and do pushups and sit-ups, or do them once you get home.

13. Switch sides

If you are usually active and social, try a mindful and calm exercise like yoga or meditation. If you are more of yoga and meditating kind of person, then try an intense and social activity like a spinning class dance class. While mixing up your workouts will help maintain your body, it's a perfect way to find a balance between being social and being in solitude while finding the lagom way in your exercise routine.

14. Plan out meals for one week ahead

Write a meal plan for a week for breakfast, lunch, and dinner and stick to that shopping list and menu. Make the plan according to your taste and circumstances and put it in writing so you will not forget it. If you want more of a challenge, choose dishes with similar ingredients so that you don't have to buy as many items at the grocery store. You can buy less and make sure to use all the food you buy, so you don't have to throw anything away.

15. Write a shopping list and stick to it

Write a shopping list and stick to it at the grocery store. Don't forget to buy other essential items such as toilet paper, detergent and so on. This will help you save time, money, and the energy not to go back to the grocery store multiple times in the week. The more often you go shopping during the week, the more likely you are to impulse buy than need.

16. Swedish cooking

Instead of going out for dinner, try cooking for yourself and eat at home. If you don't have a family who is eating with you, invite a few friends to keep you company. Try a Swedish dish included in this book. If you want to challenge yourself further, make extra food and bring the leftovers to work for lunch the next day and save some money.

17. Pack a snack

Try out a healthy snack instead of coffee and chocolate this afternoon. Prepare a nice and simple snack, like a fruit or a healthy sandwich to eat when you feel those afternoon cravings kicking in.

18. DIY junk food

Gather with your family or friends and cook your own junk food. Make pizza or maybe fries and burgers. The choice is yours. Find a recipe you like and just do it. Eat and enjoy.

19. Recycle your garbage

Gather your trash and recycle it. The Swedish do it all the time. Recycle everything from paper to plastic, and clothes. It is all according to the lagom way, and the Swedish lifestyle where you don't want to leave much damage behind.

20. Educate yourself

The Swedish apply a lagom approach to their shopping habits and how they buy things because they read about products that earth-friendly. So today, read up on environmental-friendly and/or cruelty-free labels. Consider switching over to these brands as they better your options and are sustainable, which is better for the planet.

21. Switch to a friendlier option

Try to use eco, fair trade or cruelty-free products instead of fast and cheaply made items For example, if you are buying new facial products see if you can find an eco-friendly choice or buy ecological fruits the next time you visit the grocery store. Another thing you can do is try to find locally produced products to buy. When buying locally, you are supporting your community. Farmers and small business people will love you for it.

Thank you

Please leave a review of this book. I need to know your opinion so that I can find areas where I can improve. Reviews help me and then I can help you more!

thoresen.maya@gmail.com

Other Books By Maya Thoresen

https://www.amazon.com/Hygge-Danish-Secrets-Happiness-Healthy/dp/1521864330

Turn your life into something you actually enjoy by using hygge!

Some of the simplest moments are the most precious. Stop chasing after material objects. In Hygge: The Danish Secrets of Happiness. How to be Happy and Healthy in Your Daily Life, you will learn the secrets to making your life more enjoyable and minimizing your stress. You will learn how to add coziness to your days instead of stress. Above all, you will learn to stop staring at your phone and instead make more magical moments with your loved ones.

26410148R00030

Made in the USA
Columbia, SC
09 September 2018